CW00394994

TIMES OF CRISIS

TIMES OF CRISIS

*What the financial crisis
revealed and how to reinvent
our lives and future*

MICHEL SERRES

Translated by
ANNE-MARIE FEENBERG-DIBON

BLOOMSBURY
NEW YORK • LONDON • NEW DELHI • SYDNEY

Bloomsbury Academic

An imprint of Bloomsbury Publishing Inc

1385 Broadway	50 Bedford Square
New York	London
NY 10018	WC1B 3DP
USA	UK

www.bloomsbury.com

Bloomsbury is a registered trade mark of Bloomsbury Publishing Plc

Originally published as *Temps des Crises* by Editions Le Pommier,
© 2009

First published 2014

© Editions Le Pommier 2014

Library of Congress Cataloging-in-Publication Data
A catalog record for this title is available from the Library of Congress.

ISBN: HB: 978-1-4411-0180-8
ePub: 978-1-6235-6703-3
ePDF: 978-1-6235-6434-6

Typeset by Fakenham Prepress Solutions, Fakenham, Norfolk NR21 8NN
Printed and bound in the United States of America

A note on the title Times of Crisis:
It is unfortunately impossible to reproduce the word play in the title Le temps des crises, *which recalls a very popular French song,* Le temps des cerises *(Cherry Season) written in 1866 by Jean-Baptiste Clément and set to music by Antoine Renard in 1868. It is commonly associated with a time of great upheaval, the Paris Commune of 1871, since Jean-Baptiste Clément himself participated in the "semaine sanglante" (the bloody week) during that revolution.*

CONTENTS

DEFINITIONS OF THE WORD CRISIS

Sometimes an earthquake causes just one ripple on the ground, or a few cracks and fissures in works of art, bridges and buildings. After thousands of years of earthquakes a large crevice appears in the landscape like those in Iceland or the San Andreas Fault in California. After they become visible and are printed on a map, those traces and marks both reveal and hide a giant fault at the level of the lower plates that move slowly but then suddenly break off unseen in tectonic abysses. That fault is the underlying cause of all those surface movements.

This is the subject and outline of my book. The financial and stock market crisis that rocks us today is probably superficial, but it hides and reveals ruptures in time that go beyond the duration of history itself, just like those faults in the lower plates far below what is visible in space. To access those buried causes requires that we leave today's financial data behind.

We also need to leave our emotions behind. The poor, you and me, urgently had to rescue the rich, through the intermediary of the State. The rich must have become so stupendously rich they seemed as necessary to our survival as the world itself. Today's crisis has resulted in an explosive short-circuit of a number of volatile currencies manipulated by a few experts and the globalization of concrete reality. This is where I return to the images of the soil and the earth I mentioned at the beginning. I hope this book will enable the reader to judge the situation.

Definitions of the word crisis

The verb in the preceding paragraph comes in handy. The word crisis comes from the Greek κρίνω (krino), which actually means to judge. To explain the meaning of a term sometimes helps to clarify its significance. For example: a theatre *critic* gives the summary of a play, a short one to avoid giving the plot away, but ends up calling it excellent or bad, a good or bad production, well done or poorly played; the film critic decides the film is trashy or brilliant. In so doing, he sets up a tribunal.

The word crisis thus reveals its legal origin. It involves a decision made by a jury and their foreman. The word de-cision, of Latin origin, means to cut in two, as with scissors. Yes or no, must we judge the accused guilty or not? At the end of the trial a decision is made; in the past it sometimes involved cutting off a head. Sometimes the critic's decision determines the work's success or loss of reputation.

In space, a decision becomes a forking road: we go left or right; the play is a success or failure; the accused is guilty or not, condemned or released. We are told that the young Hercules had to choose between two paths, vice or virtue. So judge and choose for yourself.

Ever since Bayle wrote his *Dictionnaire historique et critique*, and Leibniz brought God before the court of philosophers on the charge of being responsible for Evil, and also since Kant wrote his famous works, philosophy and history together entered an era where critical approaches became the rule. These two disciplines settled in as supreme judges, themselves exempt from criticism.

The term crisis has become part of the medical vocabulary, and as such has great relevance for our discussion. It describes the state of an organism confronting a growing infectious, nervous, blood or heart disease to the point where its existence is endangered: a nervous collapse, an asthma attack, an apoplexy or epileptic fit, a heart attack… In such a situation, appropriately called *critical*, the body automatically makes a *decision*: beyond the limit it has reached, it either dies or takes an entirely different path. It is a fork in the road and also a choice. If it survives the crisis, it goes a different way and recovers.

What should we make of such a recovery? It is never a return to a previous state—the term "recovery" is inaccurate—and does not restore the earlier condition: that would imply a loop-like return to the original course leading to the crisis. Recovery implies a new state, as if remodeled by the organism's new efforts. A crisis propels the body either towards death or to something new it is forced to invent.

By the way, this is one of the magnificent secrets of life: the possibility of creating automatically, from scratch, an entirely different organization of the organism! Could we, too, do something similar?

If we are really going through a crisis, in the strong medical sense of the term, then a return backwards is no good. The terms "stimulus" or "reform" are irrelevant. If we are really dealing with a crisis then no "recovery" is possible. Like a rehearsal, it would again throw us back into a similarly critical situation as in a cycle, or worse, an unstable and chaotic situation. It could last for some time and the frequent recurrence of the identical would result in similar disruptions. The history of nineteenth-century France gives us a plenty of examples in the numerous restorations and revolutions. If, on the other hand, the usual course of events resumes, then we were not dealing with a real crisis.

I too must choose: there is a real crisis today and so we have to come up with something new. Can I do this? Nothing is less certain. Can we outline other paths? I hope so. Which ones? Nobody knows yet, but in any case there is nothing more exciting than such an investigation.

I must emphasize that the new enters by force. We experienced a dramatic example in 1929 when an economic crisis little by little threw the West and the world into a war in which a hundred million died. It would be preferable to avoid such blindness. Many fear the obligation to invent and we cannot blame them. I have the audacity to delight in it. Why?

1

Six events

Ancient novelties

Everyone knows about the recent causes of the financial crisis overwhelming the banking casino; there are many competent analyses; some even name those responsible. I would be angry with myself if I were merely to repeat what the media are repeating every day.

I do not pretend to be an economist or a financial specialist. I simply think there is a gap between the numbers reached in the volatile stock market casinos and the weightier and slower reality of labor and goods; this gap, which is measurable in Euros and percentages, equals the immense distance that today separates the media-political spectacle from a new human condition. The numerical gap can help evaluate that distance. This is the aim of my book.

To measure both, I will go backwards in time and space as I did a few years ago, in my book *Hominescence,* where I tried to take stock of the new things that affected the West in the years following the Second World War, and more specifically during the 1960–70 decade. But first I must define my terms: how does one measure the newness of an event? It is proportional to the length of the preceding era concluded by the event. I will be returning to this point several times.

1. Agriculture

In the course of the twentieth century in countries similar to ours, the percentage of farmers and those whose profession was linked to plowing and pasture fell from more than half of the total population to 2 percent. This drop even became a collapse in the 1960s. And it still goes on. Even as it continues to be fed by the earth, Western humanity has abandoned it.

However, humanity has worked on the earth and lived off it since Neolithic times. This recent break can be considered an event going way beyond usual history because it ends a stretch of time that started in prehistory. We can say that in the twentieth century and especially in the years between 1960 and 1970, the Neolithic period came to an end.

Let me ask again: how can we estimate and measure the importance and novelty of an event? If indeed the measure is proportional to the length of the period it closes, then the sudden depletion of rural populations constitutes one of the most important and most unusual ruptures of the century. It ends an era that started ten thousand years ago. I will apply the same type of measurement to the other ruptures I will mention later.

At the same time, the proportion of humans living in cities goes from 3 percent in 1800 to 14 percent in 1900 and to over half in 2000. Demographers foresee that in 2030, this proportion will reach 70–75 percent. Already we see the emergence of gigantic megapolises around the globe.

What does our old history tell us about the importance of Babylon, Jerusalem, Athens, Rome, Paris, London, or Washington? Doesn't it celebrate the power of the minuscule minority that haunted those cities? Didn't most humans live outside those places and hence outside that story? Apart from the wars in which they died, my ancestral farmers and sailors, even those close to my own generation, knew nothing of that history, except that it stole their children's lives from mothers and from girls their young loves.

When the majority of humans move away from the land, relations to the world are changed. A high percentage among the generations that follow me has never seen a chick or straw, a yoke or a ploughshare, nor a cow or pig or brood. Not only have they never seen or heard a turkey or a duck, but they can no longer speak regional languages, whose sumptuous mosaic faded quickly with the collective murder of peasant infantrymen during the First World War and which later declined precipitously when local rural communities disappeared.

Sailors and aviators now follow GPS, not stars; even astronomers work on a screen. No one observes the sky to know what the weather is like, while everyone looks at the weather report on television. We believe in nature's goodness and the tiger's indulgence. And in fact this is how the old being-in-the-world of the philosophers survives. Or rather we should say, the being-in-the-apartment, going off to vacation in Arcadia, sometimes wearing shorts.

The ignorance of the world in which we humans remained so long endures today; unstable and fragile, the awakening world changes its status and becomes the third actor in politics, as we will see.

First move: everything becomes political—from the Greek *polis*, the city—and everyone is more and more a citizen. Almost no living soul lives or will live outside city walls. There are fewer beings-in-the-world. Who then will know the world as the rural people knew and practiced it? Who now thinks about the world?

Second move: precisely at this very moment, the world takes revenge and threatens humans. Nothing then can remain political in the traditional sense.

I will come back later to this dramatic reversal.

2. Transportation

Let me now consider the new human environment created by transportation systems.

People's mobility increased a thousandfold between 1800 and today. In air travel, for instance, it amounts to three thousand billion passenger kilometers in 2008. At least a third of humanity (2.3 billion) traveled by plane in 2006 and this increase continues. There is nothing comparable since the emergence of *Homo sapiens.*

Practiced for previous millennia, the parallel mobility of fruit and vegetables, wild and domestic animals, insects, arthropods, viruses and bacteria has increased in the same proportions. The distance traveled by merchandise before it reaches the supermarkets can be measured in thousands of kilometers.

In my *La légende des anges*[1], I called "New City" an unexpected collectivity that has emerged in the last few decades. Invariant in its variations, it comprises and shuffles all cities through thousands of intercity webs, in which, for instance, the largest "restaurant" in the world belongs to the most important American airline. France becomes a city with the TGV as its subway system and the freeways as its streets.

All this movement exposes the human immune system to pandemics, to which we may no longer be able to respond some day.

3. Health

Around the 1950, the availability of penicillin and antibiotics made medicine more efficient, at least for major infectious illnesses like tuberculosis and syphilis. It seems reasonable to say that this efficient medicine only really appeared after

---

[1] Michel Serres, *La légende des anges,* Flammarion, 1993.

the Second World War. Moreover, chemistry and pharmacy produced analgesics and anesthetics whose power, in statistical terms, erased the pain which used to accompany people's lives and ruled their behaviors and morals on a daily basis. Now that we no longer live with this daily pain we call its former endurance the glorification of suffering, even though it promoted exercises that helped to tolerate life's inevitable companion—at least to some extent. For example, canceling a curse that lasted since the emergence of *Homo sapiens*, generalized epidurals have recently changed the nature of childbirth, which has become less painful for women. Here is another example, a miracle actually: the eradication of smallpox by the World Health Organization in the '70s. It cured not patients but an entire illness. A global organization eliminated a universal virus.

Just before the Second World War, René Leriche[2] defined health as the silence of the organs—that is, if they were heard, they would voice the sound of pain. Today, everybody speaks of being in good shape or of well-being, which I for one define as the organs' exquisite music. In other words, before the dates mentioned, pathology was so frequent as

---

[2] René Leriche, 1879-1955, was a famous French surgeon.

to be normal, at least in the West. Later, health became the norm.

As a result, the body is changing. After the 1950s, a different human organism emerged whose new features are not yet clear to us. I still speak statistically: less suffering, fewer incurable illnesses, and fewer traces of pain on one's skin… Hidden in the past because it was dotted with scars and spots, the body is now presentable and undresses on the beach.

Even better, at least since Semmelweiss[3] of blessed memory, we started to get control over maternal and infantile mortality and with Pincus[4], sexuality, reproduction and birth. Hopefully, sexual equality may arrive some day in our still abominably chauvinist cultures. Until recently, our history books told the intolerable lie that the French had obtained universal suffrage even though only half the adults could vote.

The time of birth, the duration of illnesses or when pain reached a peak, did not depend on us; today they depend on

---

[3] Ignác Fülöp Semmelweis, Hungarian physician, 1818–65, pioneer of antiseptic procedures.
[4] Gregory Goodwin Pincus, 1903–67, American biologist and researcher who co-invented the combined oral contraceptive pill.

us to some extent. We can even perhaps partly postpone the moment of death by abstaining from fatty foods and tobacco, taking ten available drugs and practicing two different kinds of daily exercises: the useful one for the body and the other kind that is indispensable to avoid precocious senility but nevertheless so rare, intellectual exercise.

To summarize: in a world that is more and more forgotten, in a dream nature, and a mobile environment rapidly becoming virtual, bodies emerge that have little in common with those of their fathers, however close in time.

The period terminated by these health-related events can no longer be measured in thousands of years, but reaches back to the emergence of *Sapiens* itself; it no longer just extends beyond history to prehistory, but almost reaches back to the hominization process. This is why I prefer the term "hominiscence" to hominization, to characterize a new phenomenon that is millions of years old.

4. Demography

At the same time and roughly for the above-mentioned reasons, and mainly because of the slowly generalized drop in infantile mortality, the number of humans went from two billion to six and soon seven billion, most often squeezed together in gigantic megapolises. Demographic growth in 1968–69 reached a peak never before attained by *Homo Sapiens*: 2 percent. It has been declining slightly since then.

The corollary, in rich countries only, is the increase in life expectancy that demographers today evaluate at the colossal number of three to six months per year. On average, French people in the countryside live beyond 85 years. We will soon live in the company of thousands of centenarians. Only a century ago, novels by George Sand or Balzac show women barely reaching the age of thirty.

Where are the days of yesteryear?

This re-composition of the human landscape should have profoundly transformed institutions and traditions such as the family, retirement, inheritance, succession, and transmission. Does a marriage where spouses pledge fidelity for five years resemble the one where the same promise extends to 60 years? Why, then, be surprised by the declining number of nuptials? The word may remain, but covers a different reality. The transmission of property sometimes skips two generations. Furthermore, in days gone by young men used to go to war, a flower in their gun, to give their country additional life expectancy. Today, would they as enthusiastically hasten to offer a few decades to a collectivity they consider disgusting and monstrous, or to generals seen as killers? Why, then, be surprised by a totally different sensibility towards war? Would we today build bronze or marble statues on our squares for assassins that are glorified by history according to the number of corpses they sent to mass graves during their lifetime?

Where are our heroes of yesteryear?

5. Connections

After the world and the body, let us look at our relationships. New technologies change our ties, our neighborhoods, our knowledge and how we acquire it. *Connectivity* replaces collectivity. The most ignorant among us now has fairly easy access to more knowledge that yesterday's greatest scholar. This ease renders obsolete academic dissertations in history or philosophy where the scholar studiously copied all possible documentation on a given topic and displayed it to show his determined expertise. One click makes it all immediately accessible; one fraction of a second replaces ten years of research. We face a formidable deluge of details, information, observations, and data in general. As a result, together with a new concept of reason which is losing some of its abstraction, a new objective collective memory emerges, which tends to replace the subjective memory that is disappearing fast.

Where are our learned scholars of yesteryear?

What will become of our pedagogy of yesteryear?

Moreover, we no longer inhabit the same space since we no longer refer to landmarks in terms of distance. Our old address, decorated with a street number and the mention of some geographic division, showed that we were living in the old Euclidian or, rather, Cartesian space. The same term "address", derived from royal laws, allowed tax collectors and policemen to go to people's home if taxes were not paid, military service not performed, or when offenses or crimes were committed. Cell phone codes and the "adèle"—the superb cell phone code of our Québécois friends—no longer refer to networks of distance; their encoding suggests we now inhabit neighboring spaces. New technologies do not lessen remote distances but transport houses into an entirely different topological space. All neighbors now, we no longer live in the same home as our fathers.

Where is our habitat of yesteryear?

What has also changed is the influence of topics that would have been considered unimportant or even vulgar before. Two summers ago, a Walloon citizen and ordinary housewife, Mrs Huard, had more visits on the Web than the votes obtained in all the campaigns by the politician asked to form the government. A young genius of one of Montpellier's suburbs, Rémi Gaillard, makes quick, funny videos and his site gets 400 million visits, a world-scale number. He invested only 4000 Euros and made little or no profit. Here are two people, a man and a woman, whom I respect very much and who teach respect for any passer-by in the street. Indeed, I prefer their quasi-anonymity to the glory of those who want to rise above everyone else with their weapons and physical, intellectual, financial, or media violence. I like those swallows who finally announce a Spring of democracy, that ideal of which we have only known counterfeits since the lies of aristocratic Greece.

Where are the politicians and stars of yesteryear?

6. Conflicts

I chose to have my analysis go back half the century separating us from the Second World War because it marks another major date in the hominization process. It is the first conflict where, according to experts, humans succeeded in killing more fellow humans than were killed by all the microbes and bacteria encountered in and spread by the preceding confrontation. For the first time, reason, science, and technology went beyond the deadly laws of life. War for the sake of war prevailed over the struggle for life. The Bomb beat Darwin.

Before, whenever the male *Homo sapiens* indulged in the carnivore pleasure of killing each other, a battle used to bring together weapons and armies, but also rats, fleas, and viruses that killed far more than sabers and blows, or even machine guns. Although it was rightly considered one of the most atrocious mass killings of all times, the First World War provoked fewer deaths than the so-called Spanish flu, whose victims may have numbered a 100 million, according to the latest estimates. The Second World War marks the moment of reversal: in terms of thanatocracy, we now do better than nature! What an atrocious model for domination! Yes, at that moment humans became more dangerous for humans than the world.

The Manhattan Project led to the A-bomb of Hiroshima and Nagasaki, which I have called the first world-object, that is, an object one of whose dimensions is compatible with one of the physical dimensions of the world. Other world-objects have since then seen the light: satellites, the Web, nuclear waste and nanotechnologies. The Cold War continued the process and some nations, overtly or covertly, acquired the H-bomb.

The equilibrium of global power changes into a situation that is difficult to analyze. Most paradoxically, it is not certain that the stronger, or even the strongest, will remain master for long. An example: even while spending over one trillion dollars, the indisputable superpower has been unable to win a war against one of the weakest countries of the planet. This is a strange crisis of power.

Where are the lords of yesteryear?

The global crisis

Let us summarize the list. The last few decades have seen the radical transformation of our relations to the world and nature, of the body and its suffering, the environment, the mobility of humans and things, life expectancy, control over reproduction or sometimes death, global demography, virtual space, the nature of relationships in collectivities, and knowledge and power.

In one area at least, we are able to compare historical developments. The computer age offers new means of storing, managing, sending, and receiving information. Before this, printing in the fifteenth century AD and writing in the BC era had achieved analogous results. Those two achievements transformed the law, cities, government, commerce, science, pedagogy, and religion, and represent concrete evidence that soft technologies have far greater influence on society compared to hard technologies with their overvalued consequences. Mathematics is born with writing and modern science with printing. Similarly, coins replace barter and then bank notes replace coins. And so on, from monotheistic religions of the Holy Book and Scriptures, born in the Fertile Crescent, and the Reformation during the Renaissance. Such a spectrum of changes affects almost all institutions; it twice threw light on recent history and is doing so again today. We witness partial local crises that are due to new technologies and that touch all the areas I have just enumerated.

However, we have no equivalent model to evaluate the effects of agricultural or bodily mutations, nor for ruptures that concern relations to the world and other humans. Let me emphasize again that the importance of an event can be measured by the length of the era it concludes. Here, changes stop or end periods that are as long as the one separating us from the Neolithic, or even from our own emergence—in other words, tens of thousands or even millions of years. I clearly see the uphill side of the crevice but I am not sure I see the downhill slope as clearly. Have women and men ever changed more since they emerged? This is why I used the new term of "hominiscence." What happens when such decisive changes occur? When one examines each of the different components of these changes separately, it is easy to see why crises have emerged in the production and circulation of agricultural products, in education, the University, in short in the transmission of knowledge and its traditions, the army, war itself and terrorism, hospitals, the law, social relations, cities, and religions… In other words, it is not enough to talk about the recent financial disaster, whose loudly proclaimed importance derives from the fact that money and the economy have seized all power, the media and governments. It would be better to accept the fact *that all our institutions clearly and globally are experiencing a crisis going far beyond the scope of normal history*.

Tell us now that this is *not* a crisis!

Contemporary events

The decade I spoke about experienced three almost imperceptible wrinkles on the smooth surface of history.

Between 1960 and 1965, peasant revolutions broke out in France, from Brittany to the Aveyron, Alsace and the Pyrénées, which left about ten people dead, a rare occurrence today. Between 1960 and 1962 the Vatican II Council took place in Rome; its *aggiornamento* worried— or rather, threw off balance—the largest world religion, the Catholic Church. Finally, in 1968, student movements spread all over the planet while the atomic bomb became nuclear.

I believe those three events represented a tectonic plate; they reacted to the changes of hominiscence listed above. Few analyses recognized their importance, since everybody thinks in economic or political terms. Nevertheless they affected what were our ancient and deep-seated traditions and cultures: the realms of religion, culture, and scholarship, and the military—that is, the social classes once outlined by Georges Dumézil: priests and clerics, warriors, and producers. I will come back to this triad that for thousands of years had shared power in the Indo-European era.

Strangely and dangerously, in spite of those major trans- formations, our institutions, whether political, religious, military, health-related, financial, entrepreneurial, or other, continued as if nothing were happening.

These institutions were conceived, invented, and organized for a humanity of fewer than a billion souls, including an immense majority of peasants tied to the land and scattered over rural spaces, manual workers whose bodies were rarely cared for and even less medicated, and whose life expectancy was 30 years. They were subjected to daily pain, had zero comforts and survived famine and illnesses with difficulty, facing a nature experienced as cruel. Nevertheless, economic and political theories and social systems continued to manage humans and a world that no longer had anything to do with these millenary times which suddenly ended in less than half a century. We will pay for this blindness.

In other words, the gap between the real situation of nature and society as it changed and is still changing today, was continually growing in the last 50 years, creating new bodies, a new relation to the world, and different neighborhood relations. In other words, this is a gap between a new reality and organizations created at a time when humanity lived very differently. Another way to measure it is the distance between the rich countries and the others, which in my *La Légende des anges*, I compare to the differences our Greek and Roman ancestors established between mortals and the gods.

Nothing is riskier than living in this gap. It strangely resembles the tension between two tectonic plates, which silently prepares an upheaval whose intensity will be proportional to the length of the wait.

As a result, still dominant but suddenly outdated institutions, like erstwhile dinosaurs, take refuge by drugging themselves with spectacles. Yes, there is bread, the economy, purchasing power, unemployment…, bread, yes, but especially games to forget the bread, television and radio games, sports matches, even electoral games. Distressed, we witness the permanent distribution of spectacle drugs of all kinds. The West is a drug addict.

Are we coming out at the other side of this tectonic plate of un-consciousness? I foresee upheavals that are at least analogous to those ending an entire era, as for example in Antiquity when numerous cultures disappeared. Again, I have trouble seeing the downhill slope of the crevice outlined here, but it will probably resemble an unexpected rearrangement of the consequences of these transformations. Undoubtedly the easily visible, scattered pieces discussed in the above list will form a new and unpredictable global design.

In the meantime, what we observe allows us to measure the depth and extent of the crisis; it not only touches the financial markets, work and industry, but the whole of society and all of humanity. At stake here, beyond any history, is the essential relation of humans to the world.

The Indo-European decline

I have promised a second look backward in time and another wider view in space.

In Indo-European societies at least, social and political institutions developed on a terrain that had first been divided into three domains, regimes or functions: religion, the army, economic production and trade. Recently, in numerous works where he described the triad in several cultures, languages and latitudes, Georges Dumézil showed its long-term stability in myths, symbols, customs, and behaviors. His clear and thorough exposition, often representing the triad with the Roman gods Jupiter, Mars, and Quirinius, convinced me long ago. The division between the clergy, the nobility, and the third estate still endured at the eve of the French Revolution.

Depending on time and place, power was assumed in turn by a handful of priests or clerks in the name of some equivalent of Jupiter, by military chiefs, fanatics of Mars, and by plutocrats, followers of Quirinius or at least his invisible hand. We have known few other aristocracies; we have always obeyed rare and selective masters. We lived through the millenary age of theocracies; then the feudalism of the Middle Ages; and finally the modernity of the economy. Wearing ten masks, including a democratic one, a handful of people reigned: priests, warriors, the wealthy, and even experts in the ferocious and flabby science called Administration.

Except for a few theocracies scattered on the map, dangerous like terminal illnesses, the reign of Jupiter vanished around the Age of Enlightenment, at least in the West. Today we only lament its fatal diseases or deadly remains. I hope that our atrocious twentieth century, with its various forms of fascism, Nazism, Stalinism, and the thermonuclear bomb, has seen the end of the martial reign, since superpowers no longer know how to win a supposedly easy war over the weak and small.

From reading a thousand history books, we also naively believe that the past behavior of the Roman people continuously clamoring for *panem et circenses*, bread and games, was a *result* of their decadence—or at least its manifestation. Not at all: it was the *cause*. To believe that a society can solely live on bread and games, the economy, spectacles, consumption, banks, and television, as we do today, is such a fundamental misunderstanding of any collectivity's real functioning, that this exclusive and erroneous choice will simply hurl it to its demise, as we saw in ancient Rome. It would be like saying, for instance, that an organism only needs to see and eat; it would soon die because it could not breathe, move, or drink. I am not saying the economy is marginal; it remains central—but to believe that, embellished by the cosmetic aura of democracy, it is the only power will lead us to extinction.

Let me hazard a daring hypothesis here with implications I am, of course, unable to explain. What if the present crisis in turn sounded the end of the economy's *exclusive* reign? After Jupiter and Mars, will Quirinius leave his throne? Will he die for having directed and arranged an exploitation of the world fatal to himself? For organizing work that mainly exhausts him? For having divided humans into classes leading to his own overthrow? Would not his downfall be due to the all-too-human fact that a war conducted with a technique protecting the lives on one side, will always be lost against a weak but numerous force that does not count its losses in lives? In other words, to the fact that the demography of the poor will prevail over thermonuclear power but that this victory could also signal the end of the planet?

Is our ancient economic relation to the world coming to an end? Briefly stated, the unlimited potential of research, progress, or rational and technological exploitation was and is still aimed at a finite whole of concrete, inert, or living objects. To use an image, here humanity's infinity faces the world's finitude. Let us remember we believed the contrary; we believed in our weakness and in the overwhelming power of nature, humanity's finitude and hence the world's infinity. We thought that our whole history consisted in courageously and ceaselessly struggling against powers that were always stronger and greater than ours. The image is reversed: we now know that our reason, our research, our desires and will, our history and our power, even our consumption are infinite and that the nature confronting us is finite. A process longer than history, for we believed it to be infinite, is overturned and has hit the barrier of the world whose asymptote undoubtedly constitutes the downstream slope of the crisis. Clearly we are facing a *non plus ultra* necessitating at least a bypass— or, better yet, new ways. This is the beginning of an era called anthropocenic, where humans will have to make very different moves from those made by past strategies.

I return to my earlier assessment. Whether we are dealing with agriculture and the new relation to nature, transportation

and mobile things and humans, public health, life expectancy and demographic growth, space, the new home of
neighborhoods developed by new technologies, weapons of
mass destruction and terrorism, the world remains today
the common asymptote and global reference of all these
processes. This common asymptote is well known since we
have begun to evaluate its global numbers and capacities.
Everything was going toward what we thought was the
world's infinity, but everything will come from what it has
become, a finite barrier. Our history caused our problems but
will also create possible solutions, which I will outline. They
concern walls, barriers, homes, survival conditions… which
history does not usually mention.

Facing a new type of necessity, a hominiscent is emerging
whose numbers, bodies, strength, circulation, relations with
others, science, and capacity to intervene transform both his
nature and nature itself, as well as his profound relations to
things and his own humanity. Today he has at his disposal
tools or machines whose dimension or dimensions are equal
to one of the world's dimensions. Whether they be weapons
of mass destruction or mass construction, global techniques
in space, duration, volume, speed, nanotechnologies for small
things, the hominescent rises to the level of the world.

It is therefore urgent to reconsider the respective status of those two active subjects and the respective roles of this couple that have so far been considered as aggressive or polemical opposites.

2

The things of the world

A game with two and three players

Today a finite world arises facing an infinite hominiscent. A few words here to close my argument for the moment.

Let us step back. The first act of the major evolution in our relation to the world and human destiny is played out in Antiquity, where various wisdoms, even when they disagreed, all distinguished things that depended on us from those that did not depend on us. Wise men knew—or knew they should know—how to align their behavior and will with the first, without worrying about the others that they considered to be necessary. From Epicureans to my father, as well as La

Fontaine, none of the Stoics would have had the arrogance to hope one day to control climate, epidemics, or the moment of birth or death.

The second act introduces the modern age. Let us become, says Descartes, like "the masters and possessors of nature." This program maps the path of what three centuries have rightly called progress. As a result of the research and labor promoted by the initial project, more and more things came to depend on us. I have just listed some of the performances that rightly passed for great achievements in the eyes of those contemporaries who benefited from them. This was before anxiety peddlers and the children of comfort blanketed the spoilt West with waves of melancholy.

The third act strikes at the contemporary hour on the dot: we finally depend on the things that depend on us. This is a strange, difficult to manage loop. Indeed, we depend on a world for whose production we are partly responsible. As I have said, we are entering the anthropocenic era.

Like lightning, the financial crisis I started with strikes back at us. Indeed, facing reality as it is, facing the things of the world, we confront the same situation as in the economy where we depend on what actually depends on us, money, the market, work, and commerce. This is why at the beginning

I traced a parallel between the two gaps, the one I analyze and the financial one. In other words, the concrete world behaves as if we had made it; similarly, the money we mint and the projects we undertake act towards us as if we had not produced them.

Well formulated and clearly outlined, this blinding reversal points to unfathomable situations that will require deep thought. The signs we make and the world we did not make, our products and the concrete given, our reason and reality, free will and necessity, all mixed up in a strange new way, confront us and demand a different, unprecedented vision of the world and humans, of theory and practice. Now that we have finally acquired almost total control and ownership of nature, we end up being owned and controlled more or less by nature. We were going to manipulate nature but in turn it manipulates us, just like the market. It is as if a new subject is now rising up to face us. Let us examine this.

To make this loop clearer, let us look at one of Goya's paintings which I analyzed twenty years ago on the first page of the *Natural Contract*. To avoid dealing with really difficult questions, our society takes refuge in performances and spectacles: on the one hand, terror and pity, with plenty of dead and corpses to give weight to reality and seriousness to empty repetitions; on the other hand, we have bread and games, to pique our interest. We are drugged by the question: who will win? Ceaselessly asked, the question starts and promotes breathless moments of ever-recurring suspense. Who will be the winner in the elections, in the best auction, in soccer? Who will win medals at the Olympic Games? Strange expectations for an outcome everybody knows ahead of time: the richest always win, in the Olympic games as well in elections.

Goya's painting represents two bare-breasted adversaries in combat. "Who will win"?, anxiously ask the above-mentioned drug addicts. When Hegel pits the Master and the Slave against each other, and rather quickly gives the result—the Slave becomes the Master's master—as an unworldly philosopher he forgets to tell us where the conflict is taking place: in an execution spot, a forest clearing, or a sumo ring? Obliged by his pictorial mode of representation to be more realistic, Goya paints the spot: he thrusts his pugilists in quicksand. With each blow, the fighters sink progressively deeper, and their mouths, full of sand, muzzled by anxiety, try to scream for help… neither one of course will be saved and escape the hard, dense, and compact quicksand.

The game with two players that fascinates the masses and opposes only humans, the Master against the Slave, the left versus the right, Republicans against Democrats, this ideology against that one, the greens versus the blues…, this game begins to disappear when a third party intervenes. And what a third party! The world itself. Here quicksand, tomorrow the climate. This is what I call "Biogea," an archaic and new country, inert and alive, water, air, fire, the earth, the flora and fauna and all the living species.

The game with two players is over and we start a game with three. This is the contemporary global situation.

Taking into consideration this new third party forces us to make a strange exit from the strictly political, that is, the links between humans alone, and from citizenship understood as the totality of relations between us in cities. We become conscious of the fact that from immemorial times we only played games for two and only took humans into account. We believe that these perpetual duels involving a hundred negotiations between governments and unions, and between governments in international assemblies, all defending their own interests, solve or will solve problems external to their debates. These problems concern unhealthy air, water and the seas' prodigious life, fire, and energy, the devastating disappearance of living species, and so on. We trust the old politics which is essentially defined by the game with two players confronting each other, humans against humans. It used to be called dialectics, which was even supposed to be the motor of history!

Absent from the negotiations, or rather serving as their pretext, the air continues to be polluted while life drains out of the sea and species die off. Who will defend the silent fish that nourish a fourth of the poor? Air and water have no tongue or speech, so who will speak in their names? Who will represent the earth and fire, the bees and the plants they pollinate? This is a definitive blow to human narcissism: we are forced to let the world enter our political relations as a third party. Will the new game with three players replace the preceding triad, where each function presupposed games with just two players?

Biogea

International institutions in vain perpetuated those two-player games which remain blind or harmful to the world. Who will have the audacity to found a global institution where Biogea will finally be represented and have the right to speak? In a recent book, I called it WAFEL, the English initials representing the four elements and life…. Unlike the usual institutions where the nations' delegates gather, it would bring together direct representatives of water, air, fire, earth, and life—in short, of Biogea, whose name means Life and Earth.

We have always lived and will be living in that new and ancient human home. Yes, we live there in the presence of Flora and Fauna, rocks, seas, and mountains, without borders or customs posts. Similarly, Latin families used to group mothers and fathers, cousins and brothers, agrarian tools, plows and yokes with farm animals, cows, pigs, and broods. Humans were not dissociated from their world. Biogea will not do this either. We have lived there forever, before history, wars and hatreds, cultures and languages separated us. Today we return there after a period of forgetfulness. Like prodigal sons we go home. Asserting itself against our oblivion and ingratitude, Biogea in turn makes us forget our thousand networks of separation.

It is a strange country, familiar, as old as it is real, a new and old nation haunted by things, where the living are born, including humans. Ephemeral human nations carved temporary borders and made us into strangers to one another, even though water and air know nothing of these barriers. It has its own laws like those that organize various human regions as decreed by legislators as famous as Solon or Rousseau. In Biogea, they are called Newton, Poincaré, Darwin, and Pasteur.

Well known to scholars, but often foreign today to many contemporary men and their practices, this country has no rights or politics yet and has never appointed ministers or ambassadors. *Le Contrat naturel, Le Mal propre* and *La Guerre mondiale*[1] tried to lay the foundations of an emerging juris-diction. In short, those books first proposed a preliminary peace to end the warlike violence exploiting the things of the world; then the establishment of a common good opposing conduct responsible for the pollution that dirties the world. No one has ever founded a society or even a family without first drafting laws. Of course, there is no law without language.

Biogea, where humans and the world live in symbiosis, not only speaks the universal language of the laws mentioned above, mathematics, but it uses different kinds of codes, since everything, us included, is both *coding and coded.* All of us, inert, living and human things, *send, receive, stock,*

---

[1] Michel Serres, *Le Contrat naturel,* François Bourin, 1990; *Le Mal propre*, Le Pommier, 2008; *La Guerre mondiale*, Le Pommier, 2008.

and manage information. These four rules are the universals of human languages as well as codes for living beings and things. These four operations or actions reign in Biogea. Like the laws, these codes have the same name as the Civil Code or Napoleon's code. We return to the law.

With an entirely new short-circuit between natural and cultural codes, Biogea suggests another idea of so-called globalization. To be sure, globalization emerged from our mobility, and the transportation far and wide of humans and merchandise. Understood only in this sense, it proves our useless narcissism and short-term narrow-mindedness. We have globalized ever since our emergence by leaving Africa, traveling through Eurasia, sailing towards Australia or traveling alongside the Rockies and the Andes. Very quickly we chose routes to transport fruit and vegetables, silk and spice, and we followed those travelled by the Incas. We also transported our favorite animals in our tents and the hulls of our boats, as well as clandestine passengers like rats, fleas, microbes, and fatal viruses. Such expansions that have occurred for millennia will only grow with our contemporary technologies. This globalization dates from the emergence of *Homo sapiens*, but today we are no longer dealing with the same type of expansion.

The new type requires that we think, act, and live facing the world. The hominescent described in the first part is globalizing as he forges the globe and builds up his power to face that of the world. Living in the anthopocene era as a symbiot and inhabitant of Biogea, he negotiates with it and will invent yet to be written or spoken laws, whose spirit and significance will constitute a synthesis between Solon and Newton, Einstein and Montesquieu, between the laws of nature and those of the city, between the codes governing life and those governing conduct. I believe that philosophy has forever searched for the site allowing us to understand why those two words, law and code, are valid for humans and things. Here it is.

Can Biogea itself take the floor thanks to its own codes? How will it enter into negotiations with us? Can it become a legal subject?

What the world is saying, or the third revolution on earth

At the start of the classical age a legal debate, Galileo's trial, signaled the first tensions between scholars and society:

it was still the same game with two players. Let me briefly look back at this history. In his work, Galileo formulated an algebraic language to talk about an event in the world. The Church tradition had a very different language: religious, mythical, theological, whatever. Even though there was a condemnation, it did not lead to a man's death. Fascinated by the spectacle of a contradictory and pathetic debate, history and ideology remember the fight but forget its object: the fall of a thing. Nobody in those days judged Galileo for having observed or understood this. At stake was whether the divine or algebraic language could provide explanations. Again, a game with two players.

On the contrary, among the Greeks in Antiquity, whose wisdom we habitually celebrate, numerous trials announced and preceded Galileo's. Many of those who were already called physicists before Socrates were condemned on the explicit charge of dealing with affairs of the world and hence abandoning those of the city. Sometimes the death penalty was imposed. It was not a question of confronting two different discourses but of condemning the very act of observation. Your head is always up in the air, towards the stars; falling in the well, you become ridiculous, even in the eyes of women. You are not doing your duty as a citizen and you neglect the civic morality of engagement! Death to the uncommitted!

Although they were the founders of science, the Greeks made the world into the mute site of forgetfulness and treason, the suburb of banishment. So it remains. Indeed, most of those international colloquia I attend ask me to speak about the relations between the sciences and society; in other words, about current relations between certain humans and others who engage in a thousand different types of discourse; in other words, to deal with the affairs of the city. Yes, commitment, but not to the world, which remains the third excluded party.

We regress from the lenient age of Galileo when two discourses at least spoke about things, to an Antiquity that was cruel to humans and expelled the world from the game.

The hard sciences at least deal with the world's affairs while society deals with society. To please worthy people, I could indulge in a few well-known and widely repeated variations on the spectacle game of science and society. I could talk again about the tense relations between scholars and the military; about the conflicts between biologists or doctors and jurists or religious people; denounce creationism; deplore the absence of scientific chronicles in the media;

mention again the need for ethics committees; cry about Chernobyl; repeat the rumors circulating among the public about electrical waves; quote those mowing down GMOs (Genetically Modified Organism); condemn Monsanto and their criminal strategies for laying their hands on species and their reproduction; evoke the misery of surrogate mothers— in other words, talk about current affairs!

For half a century and often in solitude, I have worked since the 1960s on these problems concerning morality, the law, and politics. I have sometimes even discussed them under sharp academic criticism. I could therefore repeat at leisure and for the pleasant sake of repetition the arguments and coups of these debates, whose glare and noise are now in the forefront since the spectacle demands as many games with two players as possible.

The sciences speak of the things of the world and societies about societies; administrators and politicians deal with cities, not with the things of the world. For many people, the famous title of a Parisian newspaper[2] signifies the worldly world of humans rather than the global world of things of the world. And as countries tend to become generalized

---

[2] *Le Monde* is the daily newspaper of record in France.

cities, who in society will now look at the things of the world? In countries similar to ours, the proportion of farmers has declined from 50 to 2 percent in recent decades; who now works in the abandoned fields? Who lives in the countryside except the rich from the cities who have secondary residences in which to enjoy Arcadia? Philosophers and intellectuals, politicians and journalists, in short those who count, since they have at their disposal sites from which to send images and words, from early age were only fed on the humanities and social sciences; who then will meet with the sciences that talk about the things of the world? When some time ago I published *Le contrat naturel*, I provoked the indignation or laughter of those good people because I asked them to become a little like physicists. We live and think as if the world did not exist.

However, here is the news. While the sciences, since the Greeks and Galileo, dealt with the things of the world in more and more sophisticated and specialized disciplines, recently they have spoken together, more concretely and united with a common voice. More attentive to detail and relations, they now talk about the world as a global partner and no longer in terms of local things. They also say that the world is speaking. It is as if scholars are beginning to decipher what Biogea is telling us.

As they continue to integrate, the sciences discover and invent the world, whose background murmur is sending society an urgent message. How should we hear this new partner, the archaic ship on which we have embarked, the home of our ancestors and our descendants? For the first time we saw strange and powerful news for humanity in the image of the globe shown us by cosmonauts. I have just told of the strength and power of the world's transformations, and now we learn of its threats. Do we hear its voices or its Voice?

I will venture the hypothesis that our Western culture and history slowly began to take the world less and less into account. We spent all our lives and thoughts leaving Biogea. Even our sciences keep it at a distance by objectifying it. All cultures take the world into account, except ours. For instance, ours substituted for the ancient natural law a modern natural law founded exclusively on a supposed human nature. The Great Pan is dead, a mysterious voice whispered around the Mediterranean at the beginning of our era. The real is rational; deaf to reality, we only listen to rationality. Humans amongst ourselves, we hunker in the city *intra muros*, away from the countryside, away from rusticity, out of the hard sciences, out of the world. Only collective or individual subjects are important, narcissistic daffodils together in their field.

However, our world-less culture suddenly finds the world again as a totality, unlike the partial or localized view from all the other cultures or our sciences of the past. Our voice smothered the world's. We must hear its voice. Let us open our ears.

Ice melting, waters rising, hurricanes, infectious pandemic diseases: Biogea is starting to scream. The global world, although stable beneath our feet, is suddenly falling on the heads of women and men. They had expected it so little that they are wondering how in their world-less society to deal with the sciences that were turned to the things of the world, and have added up and measured its sovereign forces and heard strange voices. Panic time, the Great Pan is back!

And as the world is suddenly falling on our heads, we realize, hopefully not too late, that this game with two players, often taking the form of our suffering or our wars and always of colloquia and delightful scenarios, is replaced by a new game with three players. The rules have changed and urgent problems need to be faced.

The new triangle is called: the Sciences—Society—Biogea. It really is a new game for three players: two kinds of humans often battling each other, plus the world that moreover includes us. We have three relationships, not one; we have a triangular surface and no straight line. There are no men or women in this rediscovered Biogea because we had excluded it. However, at the other summit of the triangle, it acts and reacts upon us like a kind of prime mover. The summit of the new triangle acts and reacts on the others and hence on us.

Can we express what the voice from that summit is saying?

Today the sciences, overcoming their differences, are saying what the World is saying while society is still interested only in itself. Today, as society produces the things of the world and in return receives global effects on its head, who will speak in the name of the silent partner whose worrisome rumbling is, little by little, covering the deafening noise of city centers and the booming sounds of the politico-media circus?

For example, our international institutions are well-named: they are indeed nations, and so exhibit the often polemical relations between exclusively human societies. It is always a game with two players—for instance, the men on opposite sides of the fishing problem mentioned above, where each side tries to increase yields and profits. As no one represents the mute fish, their species agonize in empty oceans even though most of the poor live off fish. In these institutions, civil servants defend the interests of their respective governments, never those of the world. Every game with two players excludes a third party. Yes, the world remains the excluded third party of our outdated policies. Aren't you laughing your head off when the world's States send politicians as ambassadors to deal with questions concerning climate, the poles or oceans without mentioning their codes, while silent glaciologists, doctors of the globe or oceanographers produce exact estimates of the dangers?

Earlier I proposed the creation of a non-international, but global institution where water and air, energy and the earth, living species—in short, Biogea—would be represented. WAFEL would become Biogea's parliament. But who would speak in this silent parliament? It would be best to move to this subject quickly rather than repeating the above-mentioned arguments. I will do so soon. In any case, it cannot be today's politicians, whose irrelevance is measured by their ignorance of the things of the world and its voice. Do I have the audacity to say that our politics today is left out of the game with three players? Because of its absence, it has become irrelevant.

Revolution: Biogea as subject

The new game with three players requires very different arrangements from political ones. This is why. As soon as the world becomes a global object, it creates a new global subject and a new society facing it: humanity. Globalization today seems to me at least as much the result of the world's activity as ours. This is a surprise for us Westerners: the new global object acts like a subject. Formerly a passive object, it becomes a determining factor. We leave behind games with two players resulting from the narcissistic relations between our sciences and our societies to engage in a new game with three players, *where the world makes the first moves, more forcefully than we do.* And as an actual subject. In a few decades, the formerly passive object has become *active*. As we have seen, the former human subject is becoming dependant on what used to depend on it. This is quite a new development for philosophers of theory and practice! Now we are approaching the tectonic plate announced in the beginning.

The sciences made the world into their object. Nothing was more decisive in the Middle Ages than the invention of those two poles of knowledge: subject-object, unknown to the Ancients. Kant found another way of forgetting the Earth by making it into a metaphor or symbol of all possible objects. He decided that the object turned around the subject as the Earth turned around the Sun. Of course, we illuminated the Earth-object as though we produced as much illumination as the Sun-subject. Which Sun-King became the knowing subject? *The Ego*, the height of narcissism! Kant also called this second revolution Copernican because it overturned the earlier so-called Ptolemaic system, where the subject turned around the object, just as it was once assumed that the Sun turned around the Earth.

We enter the third of those revolutions, the one I mentioned in the subheading. In little-read texts, despised by many because they chat about religion, old Auguste Comte used to call the planet Earth the Great Fetish. What is the definition of fetish? A God, for sure, often with two bodies, a Lion-Sphinx with a girl's head, a male with the head of a jackal, surely terrifying, sometimes responsive to our pleading, but venerated by our ancestors even though they had to be aware that it had been fashioned by a woodworker or a sculptor. Those fools confused a clay object with a subject, either in thought or intention. Those imbeciles!

Not so stupid, those ancients, or else we are just as idiotic. Just look at the world. We cannot ignore that in the present anthropocene era, we fashioned it as an object out of our demography, our dishonest appropriations, our plowing and grazing, our technologies, some of whose dimensions are on a par with the world's, and our practices resulting from our theories. And here we are suddenly panicked because the world is falling on our heads now that it has become a subject! Like a fairy, the fetish terrifies us even though we fashioned it partly with our own hands. I am getting back to my earlier result: yes, we depend on what not long ago depended on us. Will the world throw us into a fetishistic age, like the Market or Finance? (Incidentally, before me, others have considered money as a fetish, like Zola and Marx, like Comte and Hergé in *L'Oreille cassée*.)

The founder of positivism also said that fetishism constitutes the first step in the human adventure. With such omens, a new era begins, starting with the third revolution. The term anthropocene means nothing else: we used to think of ourselves as the individual or collective subjects of a passive object, the world. Reversal: we become the objects of the new subject Biogea. This is why I have given it a new name. Its voice is almost as loud today as that of the social circus. Even more, while we remain the active subjects of our knowledge and practices we have also become the passive objects of the world's transformations. As doubles we now have a new relationship like a double link with alternate feedback, with a world as split as we are because as the passive object of our transformations it becomes the active subject of our destiny. This new relationship arose because as subjects, we objectivize the world; in turn, as subject the World objectivizes us. As the subject thrown under our feet, it falls on our heads and becomes the formidable residual reality that keeps us alive, transcends us and can eradicate us. Just as we need to find another word to say "politics," we must coin two more to describe this double crossed linkage of subject and object of knowledge, action and law. Neither Ptolemaic nor Copernican—our astrophysics could also claim to be neither—or both at the same time, in any case, this new situation guides our future.

Our present crisis has arisen because our cultures and politics are dying from not taking the world into account. An immense era of our history is ending; furthermore, the time of our hominescence begins. Our past will not help us much to dialogue with our new Biogean partner, whose immanence requires a new science, new behaviors and another society. Here lies the profound cause of all our movements.

We still need to listen to what it is saying, as I have just done so clumsily. I'll try to be more skillful.

3

Knowledge and conduct

Future sciences

Let me go back to my earlier question: who will speak in the name of Biogea? Of course, those who know it and devote their lives to it.

I go back to the three functions. Will power today be detached from the old triad of priests, soldiers, and wealth creators? If so, who will replace the three aristocratic bodies that in turn or even in cahoots have managed the Indo-European era since Neolithic times? Since I do not clearly see the downhill side to the crevice, I cannot answer this question.

Let me venture another hypothesis that I grasp as little as the previous one. The beginning of my essay forgot to note that the six big upheavals mentioned above were, without exception, results of scientific research and its applications: agronomy, medicine, pharmacy, biochemistry, nuclear physics, the Life and Earth sciences...

Scientists have thus shown their power to transform the face of the world and humanity's home. No one will deny that political or economic conditions were necessary to bring about these achievements, but the initial trigger is unquestionably due to inventors, followed of course by effects that rebound on their causes. Without their discoveries, there is no contemporary age.

Moreover, contrary to industrial and financial practices, only science intuits and concerns itself with the long term, since only the long term, and sometimes the very long term, can help us understand and anticipate the present. I hope my book shows this.

Can someone give me one single example of a crucial problem today, a program or future worry that does not concern knowledge? Can we develop any project without it? The only emerging countries that can extricate themselves from poverty are those that in the last twenty years have followed a bold policy of training, research, and education.

I ask again: who will speak in the name of Biogea? Scholars. I am not asking them to assume power which has been so neglected that anybody could snap it up today; they should speak in the name of things, in the language of the things themselves, to speak in the WAFEL. They should proclaim the common Good, against the Malfeasance of those who appropriated the former triad. They must define a new type of work oriented towards reconstruction and announce the laws of Biogea according to its own codes.

During the Enlightenment, they left Jupiter behind. Will they be able to break away from the military-industrial complex and cut all ties with those sectors of the economy that destroy the world and starve humanity? I will propose two scientific oaths from this new perspective.

Scholars, yes, but which scientists? The global scientific body has always had a center. From this dense and attractive place, from this germ or seed, knowledge is deployed in its totality and recruits technologies, politics, opinions, or ideologies, and even the favor of the masses. This dense place can be considered the cause of such arborescence or, conversely, the consequence of those concrete practices or abstract dreams, manual labor or ideologies. However, it is impossible to determine the direction of this influence, since here both cause and effect, as is often the case, are wound up in each other and magnify each other in the process. This cycle feeds off itself: the sciences condition the present time but are, in turn, conditioned by it.

In history, however, the center moves.

In the beginning, rigorous knowledge centered on what the Greeks called *logos*, which should not be translated—at least not here—by either discourse or word, but which originally means one of the two proportions $a/b=b/c$ and their equality. Since those original times, we use this name, x-logy, for most of our hard or soft sciences: cosmology, biology … sociology.

What Latins translated as *ratio*, and we call reason, grouped geometric theorems, the most famous of which, by Thales, associated several sizes in the same form. We find among them formal arithmetic operations, the longest and most complex demonstrations, the first algebra, the construction of simple machines to alleviate human muscular effort, a few arguments concerning social or distributive justice and finally in St. John, the relation between man and Christ concerning the unity of God the Father and his Son. In short, measures, works, the law, the economy, and religion constitute the initial kernel.

Second act: from Galileo to Auguste Comte, mechanics becomes the unifying link. To echo Descartes, science describes figures and movements; Leibniz invents power, Pascal moments and couples, and both build the calculator. After Archimedes and d'Alembert, fluid mechanics flourishes. Newtonian astronomy is called celestial mechanics. The living is reduced to a mechanical animal.

This is where technologies are centered: the digging of canals, wind and water mills, ships adapting to the rolling waves, windlasses, cranes, various hoisting machines on the quays of harbors, all levers designed to multiply the muscular power of humans, oxen, and horses. Lagrange crowns this cycle with his *Mécanique analytique*[1], and more contemporary times add general relativity and quantum mechanics.

The transition to the contemporary era occurs when in the middle of the mechanical period, the fire of the thermic motor arrives. To be sure, the so-called industrial revolution fires up molecules, but Carnot still thinks of these two sources in terms of fluid mechanics, while Fourier wants to become

---

[1] Lagrange, *Mécanique analytique*, first published in 1788.

the Newton of heat. The pivotal knowledge of thermody-namics quickly becomes statistics and ends up turning into information theory.

Third act: from Mayer to Dirac, from Boltzmann to Watson, from the thermodynamic revolution to chemistry and electronics, just as in recent genetic engineering, the center of knowledge moves towards the large populations of elements, molecules, atoms, particles... Handed over to fire, every machine works on steam, oil, electricity, nuclear, or informational energy.

Three states: the mathematical *logos*; mechanical forces; the mathematics of large numbers, particle physics, and chemistry—in short, the return to elements.

Fourth phase: surrounding themselves with a new unifying center, the Life and Earth Sciences are now taking over. I do not yet see a name to embody them and rule as their master; there is no dominant male and so long live democratic equality!

The Life and Earth Sciences (LESC) speak Biogea's own language. Today they reinvent and unite a multidisciplinary federation possibly leading to a fascinating new kind of education that would give rise to a different society. Let us invent another word for politics and become LESC-ites rather than citizens. Under the pressure of the world, a single generic culture would become humanity's. Biogea includes the world and humans, both the subjects and objects of science, and expresses their common concerns before the WAFEL in a common language. Even more, better relations with the World would improve our mutual relations.

Shifting four times, the attractor center recruits all the sciences from near or far to become interdisciplinary; it exports its concepts, dynamics and tone to all other disciplines but also creates techniques and industries, public opinion and ideologies. Probably this center will also be the effect of these effects in a feedback loop, but it does not matter since everything depends cyclically on this center and its surroundings. Its density is important to me.

The life and earth sciences of Biogea are clearly so much at the new center of gravity of knowledge that today this center refers more to all knowledge than to a particular type of knowledge; less to the single epistemology of the sciences than to cognition as such and to acts of cognition in general. The sciences show us that the world conditions our approaches to the world.

To understand this, let us start again with the Middle Ages, which invented the separation between the knowing subject that is our active selves and the objects of the world, which are neutral and passive. The mastery over things was already embryonic in this asymmetrical coupling, whose format suddenly changed the West's destiny with fearsome efficiency. The notion of abstraction itself changed, since mathematics were no longer considered the ideal; instead we extracted and abstracted ourselves from the world. The whole world turned around us, efficient and narcissistic little suns.

As all things became knowable and sometimes known, always reduced and always at a distance, they became our property. With the Renaissance, Western culture, the mother of this asymmetrical coupling and hence of the corresponding technologies and associated political ideologies, moved vertically in an advance called progress. We ceased seeing ourselves as some things in the world among others. As our practical and thinking lives became exceptional in dispensing the laws of nature, they became different from the other existing beings subject to those laws, that is to say, to our laws. We became the Subject-Sun Kings of objects.

The asymmetry of this coupling brings an end to the immense advantage, distance and discrepancy which are now turning into a disaster. We are incurring the vengeance of the things of the world, the air, the sea, the climate, and species, which are less passive than we thought, less objective than we wished, and less servile than we dreamed of. Unstable as it is, the situation threatens to be reversed. The former slave could quickly become the master's master, which could lead to another very dangerous game with two players.

Therefore we must right away effect a new un-coupling, as taught by the life and earth sciences. The latter tell us that since we are beings linked to the Earth, our lives remain conditioned or even determined by the laws of the Earth and of life.

Our royalty is tottering. We must share it. Will we become democrats? I believe that even the language of our ancient reason, which was once supreme, is tottering as it confronts the multiple and scattered voices of the things of the world. Will we become realistic? I foresee the popularity of a kind of knowledge that is closer to us, more concrete, more physical and also more modest. Will expertise finally be shared?

To repeat: Four universal operations

How can the ancient asymmetrical, very *hard* coupling be dismantled? By the second evidence that those very sciences reveal to us: the things of the Earth and life, coded like us, know how to receive, transmit, store, and manage information. I mention these four operations that I have already cited several times because nothing seems more important today. We must meditate on their *soft* character which is specific to all things in the world without exception, and that includes us. This quadruple achievement neither glorifies us as subjects nor designates us as objects. Just as we communicate, understand, speak, write, and read, inert things transmit, receive, store, and manage information. We are now equal. The old asymmetrical and parasitical separation of subject and object no longer exists: every subject becomes object and every object subject.

All knowledge changes as do practices, labor, and behaviors.

Ethics

The underlying morality also changes. At least in the West, we are used to considering the Other as a rival, an adversary, or even an enemy. We said that Hell consisted of the Others. That dialectic dominated our ideologies, our daily conduct and our ways of knowing. Ethnology and those sciences that can finally be called "human" have gradually taught us that the Other, who speaks another language or lives according to different mores, such as the Inuit or Aborigines, is more similar to us than dissimilar. Even better, that those very differences enrich us.

However, we have stuck with the old ideology, exclusively centered on existing humanity as conceived theoretically. As for the Other that has no human language, by which I mean Biogea, the totality of the inert and the living, we consider it as an object at best, and at the worst as an enemy, indeed as the Other, absolutely speaking. Conqueror or conquered: we do not know who will win, except that we know already we will lose even if we win.

What would happen if after ethnology's marvels, the hard sciences taught us in turn that we live, exchange and speak like those Others, according to the four rules frequently cited here? What a surprise! Would they in turn become human sciences of a sort?

Better balanced, more symmetrical, the new coupling of knowledge would then depend on an ethics recognized by the Life and Earth Sciences (LESC) that would be far stronger and denser than in the other disciplines.

To destroy, kill, and exploit are no longer possible, because this will definitively end up destroying us. To sign a natural contract seems less of a legal obligation today than an obvious reality to be met within and through the new center of knowledge.

Difficult and easy sciences

The language of the easy sciences, mathematics, expresses and explains facts about which we have little or sometimes no information, where the apex of abstraction is identified as zero. Mathematics' daughter or sister, computer science, describes facts where massive information is overabundant. I have already spoken of the overflow of details everywhere. The new center also heralds the emergence of what I would like to call the difficult sciences. The old ones were easy because they dealt with objects that had previously been minutely cut up, defined, and localized, and then examined in controllable models in the laboratory. Those sciences were rational at little cost. On the contrary, the new ones are difficult because they enter into the reality of the links that unite things and the sciences that talk among themselves about things. In other words, about everything that is caused and causing, coded and coding. To be sure, they are difficult and yet accessible because they are detailed, concrete, close to us, and can easily be popularized.

Under the influence of this new center, all sciences more or less begin to look like ecology, the inextricably difficult discipline that unites all the living, us included, all that knows and is known, with all the inert conditions of their common lives and the various types of knowledge that deal with them, from the most abstract mathematics to the most detailed observations. Ecology does not dissect anything: it associates, allies, and federates. It enters into details and outlines landscapes whose maps are so realistic that they mirror what they depict. More generally, the sciences today describe in detail the world's landscapes.

I have an impertinent concern: how many so-called political ecologists know anything about real ecology? Smiling, I propose to organize short training sessions where, crouching on the grass, they would learn.

The LESC also include the humanities and social sciences

As they radiate, the life and earth sciences catch up with the human sciences and renew them. The cognitive sciences, among others, also benefit.

We have finally reached the end of our argument: how can we today think about politics, the law, and the economy or even construct a sociology without referring to our immersion in the elements and the lives of Biogea? Where formerly the old North-West passage connected the hard to the soft sciences, today they overlap. The humanities and social sciences become a kind of subsection of the life and earth sciences and vice versa. We live in Biogea and the politics of that country now overlaps with ours and vice versa.

Individually or collectively, *Homo sapiens* cannot know or be known without this preliminary immersion in life's conditions where bio-geography turns out to be more decisive than history's outdated models. *Sapiens* can no longer remain outside Biogea, which in turn cannot be reduced to a model without humans.

The DNA of our most beautiful female is no different from the genes of the one woman whose secret and sovereign coloring became the model for porcelain. Conversely, *Sapiens* intervenes and puts in a great deal of effort everywhere in Biogea, both locally and globally. The crossed loops of the new interdisciplinarity envelop all humans who, in turn, envelop it.

Two oaths

I promised to end by formulating two oaths. The first one is quite old, prompted by ethical concerns; the second one is new and results from the preceding.

The reasons for the ancient one are as follows: no ethical rule could or should forbid beforehand the free exercise of collective research into the truth. When such a moral recommendation intervenes after new inventions, innovations or accomplishments, it becomes ipso facto null and void. How, then, can we have a moral law that functions *before, during and after* research?

Analogous questions were once asked by a good-willed Greek doctor, Hippocrates. In his time, only medicine was responsible for human life or death, and it became more efficient as the organism was better understood. Neither the physicist, nor the chemist, nor *a fortiori* the mathematician or astronomer, who were all devoted to truthful explanations or experiments, posed similar questions. However, from Hiroshima to surrogate mothers, from Seveso and Chernobyl to nanotechnologies, everyone is asking them today. Ethics entered medicine more than two millennia ago. In the last six decades, it is invading little by little all our sciences in different ways.

From era to era, all doctors take the Hippocratic oath at the end of their studies. It is a unique proof that a moral code and an incipient legal standard can be maintained throughout ancient or future generations. Today we need to rewrite a general oath for all the sciences, since all scholars are facing the creative responsibilities we have mentioned. As the oath is to be taken before any practical involvement, and thus emerges from each scholar's own conscience, it avoids all the delays mentioned above. Everyone may take it or not, according to his or her free will. Here it is:

> *In what depends on me I swear: to insure that my knowledge, my inventions and their possible applications not serve the cause of violence, destruction or death, the increase of poverty or ignorance, enslavement or inequality, but to devote them on the contrary to further equality between humans, to their survival, their betterment and their freedom.*

The confrontation between knowledge and ethics is another decisive historic break. Philosophy must meditate more intensively on those very unexpected conflicts between science and the law, between the common good and the truth.

Second and new oath

Let us return to the triad. Religion managed humans; pretending to defend them, the army governed them and often enslaved them; finally the economy began to rule their lives, often implacably. Those three bodies are useful if they do not take up all the space and stay in their place. Their exclusive dominance is ending.

What replaces them today? It is the democracy of easily accessible knowledge and pedagogy. Only knowledge can speak in the name of humans today, which is what the three earlier bodies did; however, it should also speak in the name of the things of the world, which is something no one can or knows how to do today. This new achievement has become essential to the double survival of the world and humans.

For scholars to speak in the name of Biogea requires that they first take an oath whose terms must free them from any allegiance to the three traditional classes. To become credible they must, as *secular people, swear they will not serve any military or economic interest.* Only at this price can they speak in the name of Biogea at the WAFEL.

SOLUTIONS TO THE CRISIS?

However, how can we prevent them in turn from becoming an aristocracy similar to those that, behind different and often deceptive masks, have ruled peoples of all times, namely the clergy, the nobility, and those with money or expertise?

Interventions and access

I do not doubt that the new house [the WAFEL] described above will forbid it. The new neighborhood spaces where we live allow us to have access to any person by cell phone wherever he or she lives or travels and by GPS if we do not know how to reach them; we can have access to any information with search engines, in particular to any text in any language as soon as the world literature will have been digitized.

This universal access can create a real democracy for the rest of us lay people whether we are commoners, ignorant, inexpert, poor, or miserable, since every earlier hierarchy was based on the hoarding of information and monopoly of rare goods: sacraments, legal rules, family genealogy, the mastery of weapons, expertise and knacks, sources of wealth and supplies, seeds, living species, property, the secrets of theory and practice... Hierarchy is theft.

On the contrary, democracy first arrives as soon as mysteries are revealed—at first by the disclosure of secrets and finally by universal disclosure. This reversal of expertise makes it possible to equalize relations between teacher and student, for example, and also between doctor and patient— in short, any relation where non-interactive, asymmetrical and hence unjust information could be transformed into power. Paradoxically today the most beautiful gold mine resides in the *data*, aptly called since they are really given, shared, and made available to all. Such universal access changes the very nature of power.

I would like to write anti-trust laws that would forbid the secret reconstitution of those little capitals of secrets, treasures whose seizure leads to the enslavement of humans, imprisoning them. Freedom consists in access.

Not only possible access, but also active intervention. Our new living space allows everyone, whether ignorant, inexpert, destitute, poor, or miserable, minors in every way, to learn, to engage, to give his or her opinion, to participate in decision-making, to share expertise—in short, to remain attentive to his or her destiny and active in the community's. A universal vote in real time is coming, which evokes the dream of an authentic participatory democracy, since equality here also rules through free intervention as well as easy access.

I would like to write stories, songs, poems, and a thousand enthusiastic texts to encourage every woman and man to intervene, in a timely or untimely manner, in every public affair, whether it is their business or not.

Interventions and access here concern information called *soft* by specialists and not the *hard* brute force of the police-man's truncheon or the nuclear bomb, the hammer or sickle.

Let me explain.

The soft

How disastrous for thought was the old morality of political commitment! Philosophers were kept busy repeating the parties' ready-made slogans, sometimes leading to crime or blindness or the search for vainglory formatted by the media. It wasted their time and made it impossible for them to recognize contemporary reality and to meditate on the problems provoked by its ruptures. Nothing hides the new better than the news and current affairs. Faced with minimal changes compared to ours, nineteenth-century thinkers promoted dozens of new political programs, including utopias and pseudo-sciences. Our gigantic upheavals of the twentieth century have produced nothing. This is the betrayal of intellectuals.

Committed intellectuals could start on the following urgent job—that is, to work on the Reform of Understanding. This leads me back to my distinction between the hard and the soft.

Biogea is hard in the following ways: it contains toxic fruit, poisons, poisonous mushrooms, venomous spiders or serpents, devouring wolves, vultures and other carnivores, predators, parasites, bacteria, microbes, viruses... Animal or vegetal, each species has at least one offensive or defensive weapon.

Homo sapiens has intelligence. He never stopped using its power, but mostly to dominate, to go first, become the strongest, to crush everything and everybody on his way and to win. With intelligence as a weapon, he conquered nature and his miserable peers in the course of a warring evolution that is ending with a victory, however so paradoxical it might in turn lead to the species' eradication. How can this defeat be avoided? By changing this defective weapon: yes, I mean intelligence. Still on the side of venom and fang, it must change, as soon as possible given the serious risks, from will to power to sharing, from war to peace, from hatred to love. This is the objective of my philosophy, of all philo-sophy, since the word associates both terms of this project.

For the adherents of political realism, the word Love will seem quite utopian and soppy. Even feminine perhaps! Nevertheless, the *sweetness* it implies not only signifies tenderness, leniency, and peace, but also defines a set of knowledges, technologies, and practices, precisely those relating to intervention and access. They quickly become more important than the *hard* techniques we use, whose praise we sing but that destroy our habitat since the industrial revolution at least and at most since the Stone Age. The three soft revolutions of writing, printing, and the computer have transformed history, behaviors, institutions, and power in our society more fundamentally than hard changes such as labor techniques.

Let me repeat, we call work at an entropic level hard: hammer blows on a chisel, steel melting, engines, or nuclear bombs. We call acts at the information level soft: traces, marks, signs, codes and their meaning. I have repeatedly mentioned the four informational operations.

From stones they became engravings.

Here too, a kind of Palaeolithic age is ending. Today an unpredictable bifurcation is taking place: it is the end of the hard and the beginning of the soft. It concerns not only the soft of morality but also of codes, the theoretical, scholarly and work-related soft; for example, as blue collar work is lessening, there is an immense increase in white collar work in production, the law, and collective activities. This soft makes access and intervention possible. We have arrived at the deep tectonic plate where encounters, short-circuits and ruptures between hard and soft provoke earthquakes.

This is the secret of my book and the crisis: the yawning gaps opening up between the stock market casino and the real economy, the numbers of our fiduciary conventions and Biogea of the living and the Earth. Those distances amount to the bifurcation between the hard and the soft and are the same distances separating the political media circus from the evolutionary state of people and societies. I promise a long book on the Soft for tomorrow.

INDEX